Learning to Read, Step by Step!

Ready to Read **Preschool–Kindergarten**
• big type and easy words • rhyme and rhythm • picture clues
For children who know the alphabet and are eager to begin reading.

Reading with Help **Preschool–Grade 1**
• basic vocabulary • short sentences • simple stories
For children who recognize familiar words and sound out new words with help.

Reading on Your Own **Grades 1–3**
• engaging characters • easy-to-follow plots • popular topics
For children who are ready to read on their own.

Reading Paragraphs **Grades 2–3**
• challenging vocabulary • short paragraphs • exciting stories
For newly independent readers who read simple sentences with confidence.

Ready for Chapters **Grades 2–4**
• chapters • longer paragraphs • full-color art
For children who want to take the plunge into chapter books but still like colorful pictures.

STEP INTO READING® is designed to give every child a successful reading experience. The grade levels are only guides; children will progress through the steps at their own speed, developing confidence in their reading. The F&P Text Level on the back cover serves as another tool to help you choose the right book for your child.

Remember, a lifetime love of reading starts with a single step!

To Violet Perl, who'll get my vote whenever she's ready to run for office! —E.S.P.

To Robert Rowe. You're a dear friend even though you trounced me in the race for sixth-grade class president. —M.S.

Text copyright © 2019 by Erica Perl
Cover art and interior illustrations copyright © 2019 by Michael Slack

Photograph credits: Cover: White House Historical Association (White House Collection); p. 4 (top left and bottom right): found on Wikimedia Commons; pp. 4 (top right and bottom right), 15 (top), 17 (top), 18 (bottom), 19 (top), 21, 25, 35 (bottom): courtesy of Library of Congress; p. 5 (top left): FDR Presidential Library & Museum/Flickr Creative Commons; p. 5 (top right): United States Department of Defense, found on Wikimedia Commons; p. 5 (bottom left): Dwight D. Eisenhower Presidential Library & Museum, found on Wikimedia Commons; p. 8: Harvard Art Museum/Fogg Museum, Historical Photographs and Special Visual Collections Department, Fine Arts Library, found on Wikimedia Commons; p. 9: Gage Skidmore, found on Wikimedia Commons; p. 12: courtesy of Mount Vernon Ladies' Association; pp. 14 (top), 16, 19 (bottom): White House Historical Association, found on Wikimedia Commons; p. 14 (bottom): Harris and Ewing, National Archives and Records Administration, found on Wikimedia Commons; p. 15 (bottom): courtesy of Library of Congress, restoration by Adam Cuerden, found on Wikimedia Commons; p. 17 (bottom): Getty Images/CORBIS; pp. 18 (top), 38–39, 41: Lance Cpl. Michael J. Ayotte, USMC, found on Wikimedia Commons; pp. 20 (top), 31 (bottom), 34 (top): photographer unknown, found on Wikimedia Commons; p. 20 (bottom): Obama White House/Flickr; p. 24: user: AndyHogan14, found on Wikimedia Commons; pp. 26, 27 (top and bottom), 28, 30 (top), 35 (top): White House Photo Office/National Archives and Records Administration; pp. 27 (middle), 29 (bottom): courtesy Gerald R. Ford Library; p. 29 (top): Getty Images/Bettmann; p. 30 (bottom): user: Hohum, found on Wikimedia Commons; p. 31 (top): United States Armed Forces, found on Wikimedia Commons; p. 32: Bob McNeely and White House Photo Office, found on Wikimedia Commons; p. 33: United States Secret Service, found on Wikimedia Commons; p. 34 (bottom): courtesy of Library of Congress, retouched by Mmxx, found on Wikimedia Commons; p. 36: Getty Images/Hulton Archive; p. 37: Getty Images/Jim Peppler/Newsday RM; p. 40: Getty Images/Tim Sloan/AFP; pp. 42, 44: Getty Images/Mike Pont/FilmMagic; pp. 43, 45: The White House/Flickr.

Visit us on the Web!
StepIntoReading.com
rhcbooks.com

Educators and librarians, for a variety of teaching tools, visit us at RHTeachersLibrarians.com

Library of Congress Cataloging-in-Publication Data
Names: Perl, Erica S., author. | Slack, Michael H., illustrator.
Title: Truth or lie: presidents! / by Erica S. Perl ; illustrations by Michael Slack. Other titles: Truth or lie, presidents!
Description: New York: Random House, [2019] | Series: Step into reading; Step 3 | Audience: Ages 5–8.
Identifiers: LCCN 2019008089 (print) | LCCN 2019008363 (ebook) |
ISBN 978-1-9848-9391-8 (pbk.) — ISBN 978-1-9848-9392-5 (lib. bdg.) — ISBN 978-1-9848-9393-2 (ebook)
Subjects: LCSH: Presidents—United States—History—Miscellanea—Juvenile literature. | Presidents—United States—Biography—Miscellanea—Juvenile literature. | Truthfulness and falsehood—Juvenile literature. | Twitter—Juvenile literature. | United States—Politics and government—Miscellanea—Juvenile literature.
Classification: LCC E176.1 (ebook) | LCC E176.1.P399 2019 (print) | DDC 973.09/9 [B]—dc23

Printed in the United States of America
10 9 8 7 6 5 4 3 2 1

TRUTH or LIE
PRESIDENTS!

by Erica S. Perl

illustrations by Michael Slack

Random House 🏠 New York

Hi! I'm the TRUTH SLEUTH.
And these are
some of the forty-five presidents
of the United States.
That's TRUE!
But I smell a LIE nearby.

Zachary Taylor—
12th president

Abraham Lincoln—16th president

This guy was president <u>twice</u>!

Grover Cleveland—
22nd and 24th president

Let's play TRUTH OR LIE
and find it!
When you turn the page,
you'll see four statements . . .
BUT only three are TRUE.

Franklin D. Roosevelt—32nd president

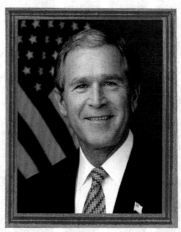

George W. Bush—43rd president

Dwight D. Eisenhower—34th president

1 Lie

Can you find a LIE about
running for president?
Go on and try!

1. You must be at least
   thirty-five years old.
2. You must be a man.
3. You must be a U.S. citizen.
4. You must have lived
   in the United States
   for fourteen years.

The lie is #2!

You must  be a man.

You do *not* need to be a man
to run for president.
The first woman
to run for president
was Victoria Woodhull,
in 1872!

SLEUTH NEWS

Woman Runs for President!

Hillary Clinton
ran for president twice,
in 2008 and 2016.
She inspired many women
to run for office,
including running for president.

Can you tell which is a LIE about George Washington's false teeth?

1. They were made of gold.

2. They were made of ivory.

3. They were made of lead.

4. They were made of wood.

The lie is #4!

They were made of wood.

It's true that George Washington
had very bad dental health.
He had many
sets of false teeth.
Some might have looked
like wooden teeth
because of food stains.

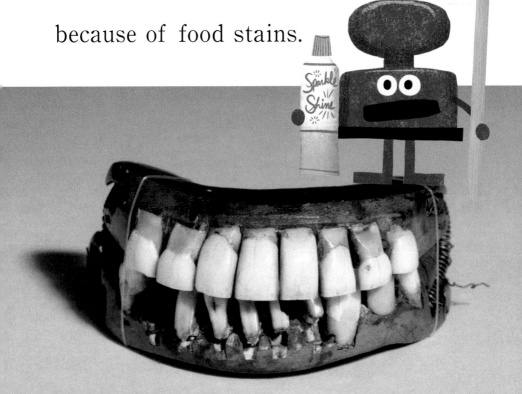

But, in fact,
they were made
from other materials,
including gold,
animal teeth,
ivory, and lead,
a soft metal.

Many presidents have kept pets
at the White House.
Can you fetch a LIE
about one?

1. Thomas Jefferson had a pet
   duck named Dick.

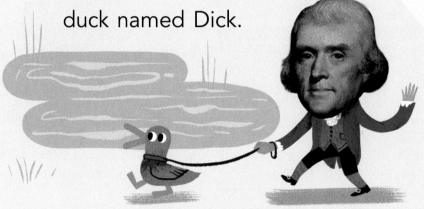

2. Theodore Roosevelt had a pet
   badger named Josiah.

3. Herbert Hoover had a pet opossum named Billy.

4. Calvin Coolidge had a pet raccoon named Rebecca.

The lie is #1.

Thomas Jefferson had a pet duck named Dick.

Thomas Jefferson
had several pet birds.
But Dick was a mockingbird,
not a duck.

Many unusual pets
have lived at the
White House.
There have been
parrots, ponies,
raccoons,
and even alligators!

Being president is hard work, but there's still time for fun and games. Can you catch a LIE about presidential hobbies?

1. Barack Obama installed the first White House basketball hoop.

2. Theodore Roosevelt inspired a toy craze: the teddy bear.

3. Abraham Lincoln was honored by the National Wrestling Hall of Fame.

4. John Quincy Adams often went for a swim at dawn.

The lie is #1.

Barack Obama installed the first White House basketball hoop.

Barack Obama loves basketball, but he didn't set up the first White House basketball hoop. President George H. W. Bush did!

There's also a White House
swimming pool.
But John Quincy Adams
swam in the Potomac River.

Is there a LIE here

about Honest Abe Lincoln,

America's sixteenth president?

1. Lincoln was born in a log cabin.

2. Lincoln is the only president

   whose picture is on both

   a bill and a coin.

3. Lincoln's Emancipation Proclamation

   contributed to the end of slavery.

4. Lincoln gave a famous speech

   called the Gettysburg Address.

WAAA!

Four score and
seven years ago...

The lie is #2!

Lincoln is the only president whose picture is on both a bill and a coin.

Lincoln is on the penny *and* the five-dollar bill. But he is not the only president found on more than one kind of U.S. currency.

President Lincoln is remembered
for writing and issuing
the Emancipation Proclamation,
which freed slaves
in some states and
helped end slavery
in the United States.

Can you uncover a LIE about Richard Nixon, the thirty-seventh president?

1. Before he was president of the United States, he was president of his eighth-grade class.

2. He resigned from being the president.

3. His vice president became president when he resigned.

4. He was a bad bowler.

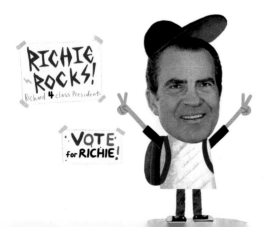

RICHIE ROCKS!
Richard 4 class President.

·VOTE·
for RICHIE!

The lie is #4.

He was a bad bowler.

Nixon was actually a pretty good bowler. The White House already had a bowling alley, and Nixon added another one.

But he is best known
for "Watergate"—
the scandal that led
to his resignation.
Gerald Ford,
Nixon's vice president,
became the thirty-eighth
president.

The Secret Service refers to
each presidential family member
with a secret code name.
Can you spy the LIE?

1. John F. Kennedy's code name
   was Lancer.

2. Ronald Reagan's code name
   was Rawhide.

3. Bill Clinton's code name

was Saxophone.

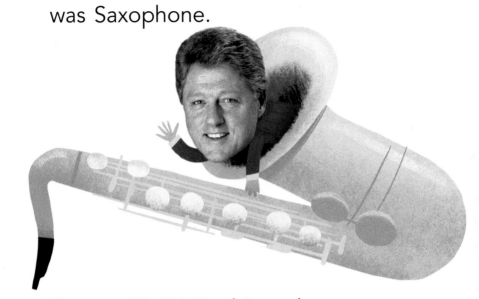

4. George H. W. Bush's code name

was Timberwolf.

The lie is #3.

**Bill Clinton's code name
was Saxophone.**

Bill Clinton actually *plays*
the saxophone.
But his code name was Eagle.

Some code names are cool.

President Obama was Renegade.

Others are funny.

Karenna Gore,

the daughter of

Vice President Al Gore,

was Smurfette.

Don't blame the Secret Service—

she chose the name herself!

Presidents come from all kinds of backgrounds.

Can you find a LIE here?

1. Thomas Jefferson was a lawyer and a scholar.

2. Andrew Johnson was a tailor.

3. Jimmy Carter was a locksmith.

4. William Howard Taft was a judge.

The lie is #3.

Jimmy Carter was a locksmith.

Before becoming president,
Carter was a peanut farmer
in Plains, Georgia.
After his presidency,
Carter returned to Georgia,
but not to farm peanuts.

Instead, he decided to
advocate for peace,
build houses for
families in need,
and teach classes at
a church Sunday school.

Barack Obama achieved many firsts in his presidency. Could there be a LIE about him here?

1. He was the first U.S. president who was African American.

2. He was the first U.S. president who was born in Hawaii.

3. He was the first U.S. president to host a Passover seder at the White House.

4. He was the first U.S. president to use email.

To: M.Obama@w_house.gov
Subject: Email is awesome! :)

The lie is #4.

He was the first U.S. president to use email.

Truth is, the first president to use email was Bill Clinton. But Obama did use it regularly—including on mobile devices, which *was* a presidential first.

Obama was also
the first president
to answer questions
from the public
by streaming video
from the White House website.

Donald Trump is the forty-fifth president of the United States. Can you uncover a LIE about him here?

1. Before he was president, Donald Trump studied canaries.

2. Donald Trump was the oldest incoming president.

3. Donald Trump's campaign slogan was Make America Great Again.

4. Donald Trump's wife, Melania, was born in Slovenia.

Is he still there?

The lie is #1.

**Before he was president,
Donald Trump studied canaries.**

Many presidents were
former elected officials, lawyers,
war heroes, and scholars.

Donald Trump was a businessman
and had a
reality television show.
Though he didn't study canaries,
he does love to "tweet."

You did it!
You are officially a
TRUTH SLEUTH like me.
Keep up the good work!

- Read with an eye for TRUTH
  and a nose for LIES.
- Ask your parents, guardian,
  teacher, or librarian to help
  you find the best books and
  most reliable websites.
- Share what you know
  and how you figured out
  it was TRUE.
- Play TRUTH OR LIE
  with your friends and family.

Remember, just because
someone says something,
it doesn't mean it is TRUE,
even if that person
is a president!

Want to Learn More FACTS About Presidents?

Books to read:

Grover Cleveland, Again! A Treasury of American Presidents by Ken Burns, illustrated by Gerald Kelley (Alfred A. Knopf Books for Young Readers, 2016)

Lives of the Presidents: Fame, Shame (and What the Neighbors Thought) by Kathleen Krull, illustrated by Kathryn Hewitt (Houghton Mifflin Harcourt, 2011)

So You Want to Be President? by Judith St. George, illustrated by David Small (Philomel Books, 2000)

White House Winners: What You Don't Know About the Presidents by L. J. Tracosas, illustrated by Josh Lynch (Scholastic, 2016)

Websites to check out:

kids.nationalgeographic.com/explore/history/presidential -fun-facts

mountvernon.org

nps.gov/subjects/presidents

whitehousehistory.org